"Regardless of your age or where you are from, Tina Siemens's book *The Little Sandals That Could* is sure to inspire and entertain you. It is not only about a family's journey to a better life for themselves; it's about the principles that they hold dear, how the bonds of family help them through difficult times, and why faith is a must if you are going to succeed. Through Tina's adventures, we're able to see the good and sometimes not-so-good side of humanity. But we also see how the little things can make a difference and keep us moving forward. A book that couldn't have come at a more important time, *The Little Sandals That Could* shows us that a little faith can go a long way."

> —By Cyrus Webb, media personality and top 200 Amazon reviewer

"What an incredibly encouraging journey! *The Little Sandals That Could* gives the reader hope even in the most dire circumstances. What a great read for children and adults."

> —By Rosie Regan, American businesswoman

"A remarkable journey to U.S. citizenship retold by the very talented author Tina Siemens. Her heartfelt words help the reader understand the trials and tribulations and the joys the Rempel family experienced. This book is a witness to the power of prayer and love."

> —Carla Gray Stringer (Ms. Gray is the third-grade teacher referenced on pages 33 and 34)

"I was deeply touched by my dear friend's personal story as an eight-year-old immigrant girl who travels to Texas and experiences a whole new world. The story is uniquely told through her prized possession: a pair of purple sandals. Get ready for your heartstrings to be pulled and also to gain a glimpse of how God sees this precious child through a life-changing transition. Young or old, the story is a must-read."

—By Julie Carter

"The story of the Mennonites in Seminole has never been told any better or clearer. It may have been written for children, but its content appeals to adults, especially those who immigrated here with some difficulty. The sad parting with a doll was written with such tenderness and is extremely touching, and her excitement of getting the purple sandals jumps from the page into the readers' hearts. Such an involved story written with strong clarity is truly a literary accomplishment. The struggles Tina and her family experienced have made her appreciate every kindness extended to her and every accomplishment and bite of good food that she enjoys. Tina points out that simple things like sandals and ice cream are the real source of happiness and satisfaction."

—By Tumbleweed Smith, author of *Under the Chinaberry Tree* and producer of the syndicated radio series the Sound of Texas

The Little Sandals That Could

A CHILD'S JOURNEY TO A NEW COUNTRY

TINA SIEMENS

Tina (Katharina) Siemens P.O. Box 211 Seminole, Texas 79360

SeminoleTheBook@gmail.com

Website: SeminoleTheBook.com

Printed in the United States of America.

ISBN: 979-8-4404-0139-6

First Trade paperback edition in 2022.

Author Consultant and Editing: Company 614 Enterprises, LLC.
Illustrator: Valerie Bouthyette
Text Design and Composition: Rick Soldin

Photo on page 76 by Loretta Walls Photography; Photos on page 79 by Alejandra Dodge Photography.

I dedicate this book to our four grandchildren—
Bryleigh Kaye, Kira Lynn, Kaden Lee, and
Hudson Lee.

Author's Note

Words in **_ALL CAPS, BOLD,_** and **_ITALIC_** are teaching
words for parents to discuss with the children.

Contents

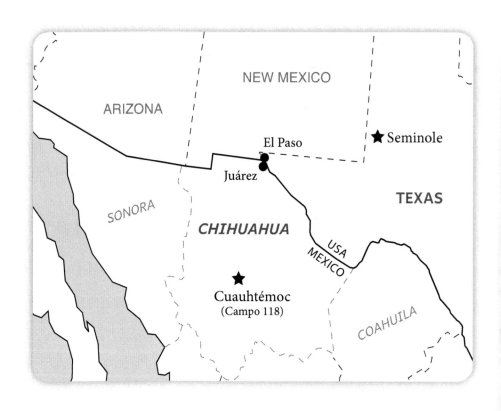

Chapter One

"Happy is he who has the God of Jacob for his
help, whose hope is in the Lord his God."
—Psalm 146:5

January 1976

Seven-year-old Tina was
excited. Today she would
be fitted for a new pair
of sandals.

Tina lived in
Mennonite Campo
#118 in the city
of Cuauhtémoc.
Cuauhtémoc is located in
the state of Chihuahua
and the country of
Mexico.

At times, the land in Campo #118 was dry and dusty. Tina
had no shoes because children went barefoot, except when
they were old enough to go to school. This would be Tina's
first year of school, and she needed a new pair of sandals.

In the Mennonite tradition, children stayed at home
whenever they weren't in school. Going to school was a

special time for children like Tina. She would get to learn and make new friends.

One day, Tina's parents, David and Anna, were going into town to do some shopping. They promised their children that they would each get a new pair of sandals. Tina was so excited that she had barely slept the night before.

Tina's father called her and her brother and sister to the barn. They each sat on a bench so their father could measure their feet. Tina waited while her siblings took turns getting measured.

Her father took his time marking down all their sizes. Tina could hardly wait for her turn. Finally, it came, and Tina stepped on the wooden ruler. But she was ticklish.

"Hold still," her father said.

Tina wiggled her dusty little toes. "It tickles, Dad," she said. Finally, her father made the mark on the ruler.

At that young age, Tina had no idea what the future held or where her ticklish feet would take her. She also didn't know that this new pair of sandals would have to last her a long time in a faraway land.

After being fitted for her sandals, Tina's parents drove off down the highway. She stood at the end of their dusty driveway and stared after them. She was there for a long time, waiting for them to return.

Suddenly, Tina saw her parents' dark green Volkswagen Beetle coming toward their house. Tina was so **HAPPY** that she jumped for joy and shouted, "My sandals are here!"

The children gathered around Tina's mother as she handed out packages. Tina took hers and carefully pulled out a brand-new pair of purple jelly sandals. She held a sandal to her nose and breathed in. "Oooh, that smells good!" Tina said. This day had turned out to be one of the best ever.

When school started, Tina proudly wore her sandals everywhere. She met new friends and showed them her sandals. They loved the color.

One day, Tina's parents told her the family was moving to a new land.

"Can I take my sandals?" Tina asked.

Her father nodded. "Yes, but your doll will stay behind. There's not enough room."

Tina cried. Not only would she have to leave her friends behind, but she'd even have to say goodbye to her only doll.

"Don't worry, Tina," her father said. "We will carefully pack away your doll, and someone else will bring it to us."

"Where are we going?" she asked.

"To America. To a place called Seminole in the state of Texas. Now go to your mother and get ready."

Tina's mother put her in a brand-new dress, which she'd sewn especially for Tina. Then she pulled Tina's hair back tight, braiding it so the strands wouldn't come undone. When she was finished, her mother dabbed sugar water on her hair. This acted like hairspray and kept the braids in place.

Tina felt her forehead. It ached because the hair was pulled so tightly.

"Come on, children, let's go!"
her mother called.

Tina ran to their
barn and found the
box where her doll
was packed. She
lifted the doll and
kissed it goodbye.
"Don't worry," Tina said,
"someone will bring you
back to me soon. Then we'll be
together again." Tina imagined the
doll smiling back at her, like she understood.

A pickup truck with a camper shell pulled into their yard.
"Okay, children," Tina's father said, "everyone get in the
back of the truck."

Tina joined her family as
well as another family, the
Schmitts, in the back of the
truck. They were all going to the
same new land.

Tina saw her mother cry as
she looked at their house. It
was sad to leave everything
behind that they'd called
home.

As the truck pulled away,
Tina took one last look at all her

favorite places. There was the large tree where locals traded fruit and fish for the Mennonites' cheese, eggs, and butter. A small cart selling popsicles, called *paletas* in Spanish, had children around it, waiting for their sweet treat. In Tina's memory, she could see herself and her brother, David, standing in front of this cart waiting for their paleta.

They passed her great-grandparents' house, then her grandparents', then her friends'. The houses disappeared when the pickup truck drove over the hill and headed down the road. Tina pulled off her sandals and held them close to her chest.

Her life in Mexico was over forever.

Chapter Two

"Lying lips are an abomination to the Lord, but those who deal truthfully are His delight."
—Proverbs 12:22

March 1977

Tina and her family drove and drove. She saw parts of Mexico she'd never seen before. With every mile they traveled, she missed her doll more and more.

After many hours crammed in the back of the pickup truck, Tina and her family finally arrived in Juárez. Juárez is a town in Mexico on the border of the United States of America. Her father got out and walked to an office where the other Mennonite men were gathered. They needed visas to enter the United States.

As Tina, her mother, and siblings, along with the Schmitts, waited in the truck, the air turned hot. Finally, they rolled down the windows and took a nap. Waiting made them tired.

Her father returned with bad news. "The lawyer did not show up with the papers. The office closed, so they made us leave. We must find a place to stay for the night."

"Will we have to come back tomorrow?" Tina's mother asked.

"Yes. I'm sure the lawyer will be here tomorrow."

They drove to a small motel. It wasn't fancy, but it still cost money, something Tina knew they didn't have a lot of.

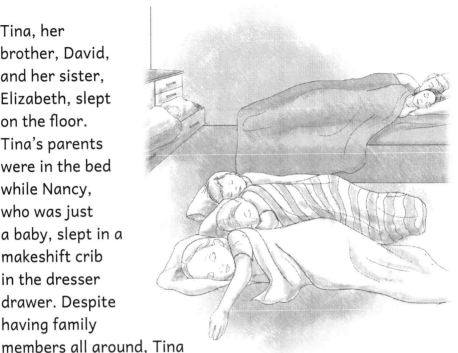

Tina, her brother, David, and her sister, Elizabeth, slept on the floor. Tina's parents were in the bed while Nancy, who was just a baby, slept in a makeshift crib in the dresser drawer. Despite having family members all around, Tina had trouble sleeping.

The following morning, Tina's father dressed and left to go back to the immigration office. Everyone else stayed at the motel.

Without her doll, there was nothing for Tina to do. She decided to explore the halls of the motel, looking for something to play with. She found a closet in the hallway with red writing on the door. Tina couldn't resist. She opened the door.

Inside, she saw a metal box with a red handle. Tina wondered what the handle was for. Standing on her tiptoes, she reached up and pulled the handle down. Suddenly, the light in the closet went out.

Tina peeked out the door and saw that the hall was also dark. She crept out of the closet and saw that the lights had gone out in the entire motel. Because she was curious and wanted to know what the big, red handle did, Tina had shut off the electricity for the entire motel.

A manager came running and found Tina standing near the closet. He was very upset. He grabbed Tina's arm and marched her back to the room, where her mother was frantic, waiting in the dark. Her mother couldn't understand what the manager was saying, but he was very upset, and Tina noticed that his face was the same color as the handle that Tina had pulled.

When Tina's father returned that evening, he was not happy. The lawyer had not come with the papers. This meant her father did not have the visas they needed to enter the United States.

Tina's mother told her father about her bad behavior, and he told Tina that for punishment, she would have to stay in their room alone.

While her family was visiting with the Schmitt family, a thunderstorm erupted. Lightning and heavy thunder scared Tina. She said out loud that she would never again go where she was not allowed, even if she was curious.

Tina's family came back to their room, but Tina was still sad. She didn't like being in a motel in Juárez, and she missed her doll.

But at least Tina had her sandals. And the children of the other families played with Tina and her siblings in the long hallways. That took her mind off her sadness.

After four long days in Juárez, Tina's father had still not seen the lawyer. He was very worried. He and Tina's mother prayed silently. They asked God for help.

On the fifth day, her father went back to the immigration office. By late in the afternoon, he still had not found the lawyer.

Finally, an immigration officer motioned for him to come to the counter. Speaking in Spanish, he asked David why he was there. Tina's father decided he would tell the truth no matter what. He had heard from some other men that if he lied, he could get papers to enter the country. But Tina's father knew *LYING* was wrong. If he couldn't enter the United States honestly, he wanted no part of this new land.

Tina's father replied in Spanish that he and many other Mennonites had bought property in Texas. They were all waiting for paperwork from a lawyer so they could enter the United States.

The immigration officer listened and nodded. Then the officer grabbed some papers and began stamping them. To Tina's father's surprise, the man handed him the visas they needed to enter the United States.

Honesty had worked. So had praying to God for help. Tina's father couldn't wait to get back to the motel and tell his family. There would be a joyous celebration.

The dusty, dirty pickup truck rumbled along the Texas highway, passing over the Guadalupe Mountains. For hours they traveled as the sun dipped below the horizon.

As dusk arrived, Tina fell asleep.

Sometime later, Tina's brother nudged her arm. "Wake up," he said. "Dad has something to say."

The pickup truck climbed a small hill. When it reached the top, her father pointed excitedly at the lights ahead. "There it is!" he cried.

Everyone stared out the windshield, looking at the lights of Seminole.

"We're home!" he said. "Now, we're home!"

Chapter Three

"This is the day the Lord has made; we
will rejoice and be glad in it."
—Psalms 118:24

When Tina woke up the following day, she rubbed her eyes. She was in a strange place. It was called the TeePee Lodge. The TeePee Lodge was a motel in the town of Seminole. It would be her new home for a while.

Tina's father went outside and gave money to the man who had driven them to Texas. Then the man got into the pickup truck and drove back to Mexico. Now Tina's family would have to walk everywhere.

"Let's go eat breakfast," her father said as he clapped his hands.

Tina dressed and put on her purple sandals. She was excited to see this new town.

The entire family walked down the sidewalk to Jo's Café. Tina didn't know what a café was, but there were some delicious smells coming from it.

Inside the restaurant, the family found a table in the back. Because the menu was in English, they couldn't read it, so they relied on the pictures on the menu. In this way, Tina's father was able to order breakfast for everyone.

When the food arrived, it was hot and fresh. Delicious butter and jams were spread on the toast, and there was plenty of salt and pepper for the eggs and sausage.

Tina ate until she was full. This place called Seminole wasn't so bad.

Tina's family **REJOICED** over the blessings from God they had received. None of them could guess that this was the calm before the storm.

After breakfast, her father walked a few blocks to speak to some other Mennonite men. They were ready to get on their land and start farming it, but no one knew the location.

When Tina's father finally learned where their land was, he couldn't work it until it had been divided among the families.

To make things worse, her father needed more money to pay a lawyer who was needed to make sure they would be able to stay in the United States. Without permanent papers, Tina's family would have to go back to Mexico.

"When can I see my doll?" Tina asked her father.

Her mother blinked her eyes and told Tina to let him rest. "Your father has a lot to think about. Your doll will be here soon enough."

Tina rewashed her purple sandals. She wanted to keep them looking nice because she was walking everywhere in them.

Being curious in this new land, Tina learned every hiding place at the TeePee Lodge. It was small, so there weren't many. Finally, her mother decided to put Tina to work.

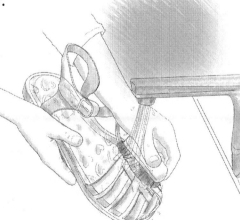

"Here, help me with the washing."

Together, they scrubbed the clothes in the bathtub, using soap from the motel. After rinsing the soap from the clothes, Tina and her mother placed them to dry over some bushes outside. It was the only place they could hang them.

To save space in the pickup, they had each brought only one extra set of clothes. That's why they had to do the laundry every day.

One day, Tina had just finished putting the clothes on the bushes when the motel manager came running up. He spoke in English, but neither Tina nor her mother could understand what he was saying.

Another Mennonite who understood some English explained that the manager was upset that they were using the bushes to dry the clothes.

"What are we supposed to do?" her mother asked.

The manager said they had machines to dry the clothes.

"How does a machine do that?" her mother asked.

Together, they followed the manager to a room with square, white boxes. The manager took the wet clothes and put them inside one of the boxes. When he put a coin in the slot, the machine turned on. Hot air started drying the tumbling clothes. Tina's mother was amazed. She had never seen anything like it.

"First, the Americans build small houses for their dogs. Now they have machines to dry clothes. What will they think of next? A machine to wash dishes?"

Later that afternoon, another Mennonite came to the TeePee Lodge with several cans of food. He gave one to Tina's mother. She opened it up and tasted the meat and beans.

"This is very good!" she said.

Tina and her siblings tried some. Even though they couldn't pronounce it, they grew to like Beanee Weenees. With purple sandals on her feet and good food to eat, Tina couldn't imagine a better place on Earth than Seminole, Texas. Life was good.

Chapter Four

"Train up a child in the way he should go, And when he is old he will not depart from it."
—Proverbs 22:6

Tina's father got up each morning, had a small breakfast, and left to find work. There were so many Mennonites looking for work that it was hard to find a job. But God blessed Tina's father. He found jobs plowing the fields of others and moving irrigation pipes. Sometimes, he worked in construction, building homes.

At night he returned, tired and dusty. Tina's mother made a small meal for her husband. They had very little money to buy food because they needed every penny for the immigration lawyer.

Through days and days of hard work, Tina's father made enough money to buy a car. He bought an old, brown Buick from a woman named Rose. Unfortunately, it took all the money he had—$200. After that, there was no money left to feed his family. They would have to make their small food supply last until he could earn more.

As he drove the car home, the sun hit his eyes. When he lowered the visor, a twenty-dollar bill fell into his lap. Incredibly, he now had money to feed his family. God had blessed him once again.

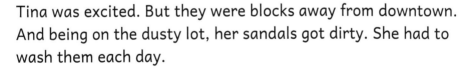

Life in Seminole was tough for Tina's family. Her father worked very hard until they could afford to rent a small mobile home. Then finally, they left the TeePee Lodge and moved into their own home.

Tina was excited. But they were blocks away from downtown. And being on the dusty lot, her sandals got dirty. She had to wash them each day.

To pass the time, Tina helped her mother with the chores. She loved helping her mother.

Once a week, Tina washed her long hair. After drying it, her mother twisted two braids, pinning the braids up on the back of her head. Every young Mennonite girl had her hair tied up the same way.

Tina's father was always worried. He barely made enough money to pay the rent and buy food. And he had to pay for gas for the Buick. It was a hard life, but there was no going back to Mexico, where life was much harder.

Sometimes her father had to give money to a group of Mennonite men in town. The money went to a lawyer who was trying to get papers to keep them in the United States. If they didn't get that paperwork, they would all have to leave.

One night, Tina's parents gathered them all around the table. Her father's face was serious. "Children, I have found a cotton field owner who needs help hoeing. The man who owns this field will pay each of you $1.25 per hour to hoe the weeds."

"I will go wlth you sometimes," Tina's mother said. "But you three children will go every day. There may be other families working in the field too. No matter what, we always expect you to do your very best."

"When do we start?" Tina's brother, David, asked.

"Tomorrow morning."

The children nodded.

"We want you to get some sleep," her father and mother said. "It will be an early start."

Tina washed her sandals and put them in the bed next to her. Then she climbed in, slipped under the covers, and fell fast asleep.

23

It was dark outside when her mother came into her room. "Tina, it's time to get up."

Tina dressed and put on her sandals. Her mother gave the children a glass of milk and a cookie. That was their quick breakfast. When they finished, they piled into the Buick with their father and took off in the darkness.

Her father pulled up to the cotton field and got out. He gave the hoes to his wife, Anna, and the children to work the field. Then he handed them glass bottles of water and a bag of sandwiches.

"You will work all day, but you can take a break at lunch," her father said. "I will be back around six."

As their father pulled away in the Buick, Anna and the three children walked quietly in the shadow-gray light into the field. Now it was time to work.

The hours ticked by as the sun rose higher and higher in the sky. It was hard, hot work. Tina grew tired. But her family needed the money. She had to keep working, or they might not get paid. And her father needed the money to pay the lawyer to get the paperwork so they could stay in Seminole.

Tina's parents were sad that their children had to work so hard in the fields, but they all had to help if they were going to make their American dream come true. And it was important for Tina's parents to **TRAIN** their children to help out whenever they could.

Finally, at noon, her mother led them to some tumbleweed bushes where there was a tiny bit of shade. They ate soggy sandwiches and drank their water. Then, after a brief nap, they got to their feet and walked back into the fields. Tina wondered how long she could go on.

Chapter Five

*"When they had read it, they rejoiced
over its encouragement."*
—Acts 15:31

Four weeks later, the sun was even hotter. This turned the land dry and dusty.

Six days a week, Tina and her siblings got up in the darkness and were driven to the cotton fields. Row after row, they hoed stickers and pigweeds, also known as Amaranthus. The rows of cotton plants, stickers and pigweeds never ended.

Tina's sandals were covered with sand. She could barely see the purple color. It was so hot it felt like the rubber would melt.

With the sun beating down on her neck, she got a bad sunburn. Yet, she couldn't stop. They had to eat and pay rent. Plus, they had to keep paying the lawyer. Would it ever end?

That evening, Tina's father picked them up and took them home. As she waited for her turn to take a bath, the skin on the back of her neck burned like it was on fire. Her arms ached, and her legs were tired.

When she finally slid into the bathtub, her sandals shed the sand that had been packed into the bottom of her soles. The hot water stung her neck. Tina was so miserable she started crying.

"What's wrong?" her father asked as he knocked on the door.

"I have sand on my neck, but it's so blistered that I don't know how to wash it off. It hurts!"

"Listen, if you hurry up, I'll take you to the grocery store and get some ice cream for everyone."

Tina sat up, her tears drying up. "Ice cream?" That was all the **ENCOURAGEMENT** she needed.

"Yes, but you need to be done quickly."

"Okay, Dad!" she squealed. "I'm washing up."

It was a miracle. Instantly, Tina felt better.

They took their beat-up old car to the H&D Grocery Store. Her father bought a gallon of ice cream and brought it home. As soon as the gallon bucket hit the table, Tina and her siblings dove right in. The ice cream tasted wonderful. In this moment, Tina forgot all her problems.

"Feeling better?" her dad asked.

"Yes, Father," she replied. "I could eat ice cream for every meal."

With the money Tina and her siblings earned, her mother could afford to buy more food. So they had plenty cans of Beanee Weenees, green beans and pork and beans. For sandwiches, they had bologna on two slices of homemade bread. Sometimes, they had a piece of cheese on their bologna sandwiches.

Tina's mother was a good baker. She made fresh bread and rolls that everyone loved.

With ice cream as an encouragement and so much good food to eat, Tina liked this new country more and more. She didn't want to leave it.

At the end of summer, a relative was driving up from Mexico with more of their belongings, including her doll, or so she thought. She couldn't wait.

One afternoon, her uncle Jake and his family arrived. Tina ran outside to greet them. "Did you bring my doll?" she asked.

"Hello, Tina," Uncle Jake said. "I have two boxes of things in the back that your father can sort through."

The rest of Tina's siblings surrounded their aunt and uncle. It took him an hour to unpack his station wagon and bring the boxes inside.

Tina's father went through the items in the box. Then a few minutes later, he knelt down to talk to her.

"Tina," he said, gritting his teeth, "I have some bad news."

Tina's lower lip quivered. "Where is my doll?" she asked.

"She's gone," he told her. "I'm sorry, but your cousins got into the box and played with all the toys. They broke your doll."

Tina cried and cried.

"If we get to stay here, I'll buy you a new doll," her father said.

"But I want my old doll," Tina cried. "We were best friends."

"I know, I'm very sorry."

Tina went to bed sad.

All she had left were her purple sandals. And no ice cream would cheer her up this time. Her doll was gone forever.

Chapter Six

"And now abide faith, hope, love, these three;
but the greatest of these is love."
—1 Corinthians 13:13

Tina heard a knock at the door of their mobile home. A man stood there. Tina had seen him before. He was an Englander (American) who had hired her father to plow his fields. He said something in English to a man with him, then left.

"What did he want?" Tina's mother asked.

Her father looked down. "He said that this is one of the driest years ever. It looks like the crops are lost. He's giving up and doesn't need the children or me any longer."

Tina's father sat down in a chair and rubbed his head.

"Do we have to work the fields tomorrow?" Tina asked.

"No," he replied.

Tina smiled.

"But now you can go to school," he added.

Tina's smile turned into excitement. She was so happy.

The following day, her father showed them where to stand. Soon, a big, yellow bus rumbled down toward their mobile home and stopped in front of them. Its large door opened so Tina and her siblings could climb on. When the door closed, she waved goodbye to her mother, father, and sister Nancy.

Tina felt her hair. Her mother had pulled it back tight and covered it with sugar water. Not a hair was out of place.

When the bus stopped, the other kids jumped off and walked to their classrooms. A gentleman had to show Tina and her siblings where to go. It was scary for all of them.

Because Tina could not understand what anyone was saying, she didn't know what to do.

Finally, a friendly third-grade teacher, Mrs. Gray, took her to the back of the room and showed Tina how to wash her hands before walking to a desk. At least she was clean for class.

At recess, Tina went outside. She was lonely with no one to talk to.

The schoolchildren moved around the playground. Three boys approached Tina and made fun of her, laughing and pointing. One boy came close and kicked her in the shin.

Tina fell, crying and grabbing her leg. The boys came closer and laughed even more.

When the bell rang, Tina stayed outside crying until the students were all inside. Then she went into her classroom. Mrs. Gray spoke, but Tina couldn't understand her. A few minutes later, Mrs. Gray brought her out into the hall. There were the three boys, looking scared.

Tina stood there while Mrs. Gray raised a wooden paddle and swatted the three boys.

The boys tried to stop their tears but couldn't. From then on, they didn't bother Tina.

After some time to adjust to school, Tina passed the cafeteria on her way to the bus. She saw the line of children and wondered what was going on. Through an act of **LOVE** from a student, Tina learned how to buy ice cream for ten cents. It was a big treat. This made school seem so much better. She even forgot the pain of being kicked in the shin.

When school was over, Tina and her siblings climbed back on the bus and were dropped off in front of their mobile home. School in the United States was much different than in Mexico.

At dinner, her father looked worried. Despite paying lots of money to the lawyer, a different bus was coming to take all the

Mennonites back to Mexico. The land they had purchased was lost. With very little money, they would have to go back and live in worse conditions than before. It was a sad time for Tina's family.

Chapter Seven

"Therefore I say to you, whatever things you ask when you pray, believe that you receive them, and you will have them."
—Mark 11:24

Each week, there was a special treat for Tina. She could attend the temporary, one-room church and Sunday school. She loved them both.

Every Saturday night, Tina would wash and dry her hair. Then her mother would pull it back and apply sugar water. Afterward, Tina cleaned her sandals and laid out a fresh dress. She wanted to look her best on Sunday.

The church they attended was close, so they just walked to it.

The Sunday school teacher was a Mennonite. She spoke Low German. Tina had no problem understanding the teacher.

During one of the Sunday school lessons, Tina learned how to pray. She had always joined in with her family in High German as they said the same memorized prayer before each meal and bedtime, but they had never prayed as if talking directly to a friend.

After the food was set on the table and everyone had taken their places, they bowed their heads. Silently, in High German, they each prayed, *Segne Vater diese speise, uns zur kraft und Dir zum Preise. Amen.* (Father, bless this meal for my strength and to Your praise. Amen.)

But her teacher explained that Tina could pray for anything she wanted any time of the day or night. Even though it was exciting to think about praying like this, Tina had never done it before. Maybe one day she would.

In the afternoons, around four o'clock, her mother held a *faspa*. A faspa was a Mennonite coffee break. First, her mother put out some bread, pickles, cookies, and other treats. Then she sat down with her children and enjoyed a cup of coffee. This was a time when Tina and her mother could talk about anything. Tina loved spending faspas with her mother.

It was Saturday night again. Tina spent a lot of time cleaning her purple sandals. They were still beautiful.

When she was done, she put the sandals in a safe place. She was so excited that she could hardly sleep. At least she was ready to go to church the next day.

Out in the living room, her mother and father were sad. They had received papers in the mail telling them they would have to leave the United States. This worried David and Anna.

The next morning, it was time for church. Tina's parents got up and gathered everyone for breakfast. Tina ate a simple meal with her family.

After breakfast, her parents dressed first and then helped the children get ready. When everyone was dressed, they headed for the door.

"Wait!" Tina cried. "I can't find my sandals."

Her father stood there, holding the door open. "Come on, Tina. Get your sandals, and let's go."

Tina ran through the small two-bedroom mobile home, looking everywhere for her precious sandals. It didn't take long for her to see that they were gone.

"My sandals are not here," she said.

"They have to be here," her father said. "You cleaned them last night. And no one has left this mobile home until right now."

"I know," she cried. "I just can't find them."

"Well, you aren't going to church in your bare feet. So, until you find your sandals, you'll have to stay home."

"But I want to go with you," Tina cried.

"If you find them, you can catch up." He closed the door, and they began walking to the church.

Tina ran to the window and watched as her family walked away from their mobile home. In a few minutes, they would be at the church. Tina had to find those sandals.

She went back through the place, looking and looking. She didn't find them.

As she went to the living room, she cried. Her family was almost at the church. Then she remembered what the Sunday school teacher had told her. "You can **PRAY** for anything you want, any time day or night."

Out of desperation, Tina dropped to her knees and clasped her hands together. "Dear Lord, please help me find my sandals."

She had not quite finished her prayer when it hit her. Tina jumped up and ran to her mother's closet. She found her purple sandals, clean and safe between two blankets, just as they had been Saturday night when she placed them there.

Tina put on her sandals and raced out of the mobile home. She ran hard and fast through the dusty land. The moment her family reached the church, Tina caught up to them.

"You made it!" her father said. "I knew you'd find them."

Tina smiled. She knew God had answered her very first prayer.

Chapter Eight

"Oh, give thanks to the Lord! Call upon His name; Make known His deeds among the peoples! Sing to Him, sing psalms to Him; talk of all His wondrous works!"
—Psalms 105:1–2

November came to Seminole. It was cold and windy. Work was hard to find.

They didn't have much money, so food was scarce. And the papers they had received in the mail told them to leave the country by a specific date. So, all the Mennonites in Seminole were worried.

A lady came to their mobile home and said something to Tina's mother. When the lady left, her mother told the rest of the family, "We have been invited to attend a church in town tomorrow. They are having a big meal and want us to come."

"What church is it?" Tina's father asked.

"The First Baptist Church of Seminole."

"Why are they having a big meal?" Tina's sister, Elizabeth, asked.

"It's something they call Thanksgiving. It's a holiday in this country."

Tina's parents discussed this invitation. They didn't know much about this church, but the thought of having been invited to it was an honor.

"Are we going?" Tina's brother, David, asked.

"I guess we will," Tina's father said.

"What do we wear?" Tina asked.

"Since it's a church, let's dress for church."

The entire family talked about what this Thanksgiving Day might be like. Hopefully, they would like the food.

The following day, her mother was braiding Tina's hair when her father came in from work and said, "You know that we are in America now, and we need to look like Americans. From here on out, our daughters don't need to have their hair braided like this anymore."

"Elizabeth's too?" her mother asked.

"Yes! Take her braids out."

Hearing this, Tina jumped up with such enthusiasm, as if the little purple sandals gave her an extra boost.

Her mother loosened the braids, and Tina's hair fell to her shoulders. Tina felt the skin on her forehead relax. What a treat! Her head no longer ached, and she could breathe easily.

Once they had dressed in their Sunday best, the entire Rempel family hopped in the old Buick and took off for downtown Seminole.

It didn't take long to get there. The large church was easy to find.

After they parked, Tina's family slowly walked to the main entrance, unsure what would happen. They were greeted by friendly people, including the Reverend Gerald Tidwell. "Come on in," he said. By now, Tina could understand a little English.

As they were led to the auditorium, the aroma of fresh food hit their noses. It made all of them hungry.

Tina followed her father. When they stepped into the great hall, there were tables of food everywhere. The Mennonites had never seen such a thing. It was something special.

Tina's family stood in one spot until Reverend Tidwell bowed to give **THANKS**. Then he picked up a plate and showed them how to serve themselves the food. Tina and her family were scared at first, but soon piled their plates high. As they walked back to a table, Tina couldn't believe she could eat all the food she wanted. It was the best evening in Seminole yet!

The Rempels ate and ate until they were full. When the feast was over, the ladies at the church showed them how to pack up some food to take home.

"Here, use these doggie bags," the lady said to Tina's father.

Her father took the bags and filled them with extra food to take home. "Don't tell them we don't have a dog at home," he whispered. "We'll enjoy this food ourselves."

"I can't believe they would give such good food to their dogs," her mother said. "This country surprises me each day."

When they arrived home, they called up some friends who had been too scared to go. When Tina's mother showed the friends what they had brought home, the friends couldn't believe it. Her mother shared some of the food with the friends. They had another great meal.

Chapter Nine

"Beloved, you do faithfully whatever you do
for the brethren and for strangers."
—3 John 1:5

It was an unsettled time for the Mennonites. They had been told to leave Seminole several times, and just before each deadline, an extension was granted. But this time, it seemed permanent. The Border Patrol buses were coming for them, and there was nothing they could do to stop them. Would all the money they had given to the lawyer come to nothing?

Tina's father spent a lot of time downtown. He met with other Mennonite men, trying to find a way for them to stay in Seminole. One man, an Englander, was working hard to keep them in Seminole. His name was Mayor Bob Clark.

MAYOR CLARK

Mayor Clark had lived in Seminole for many years. He saw how hard the Mennonites worked. Gaines County needed good workers. There was plenty of land but not enough people to farm it.

Mayor Clark talked to the newspaper reporters. Soon the town was full of reporters, all snapping photos of the Mennonites. They even came to the Mennonites' churches and Sunday schools, taking pictures of the children. The reporters couldn't get enough of the women's dress, especially their colorful scarves and hats. The Mennonites didn't know what to think about this.

One evening, Tina's father came home upset. He had learned that the only way they could stay in America was for its government—Congress—to pass a special bill and grant the Mennonites citizenship. This was so hard to do that Americans often said, "It'll take an act of Congress" when they thought something was impossible.

"What chance do we have of getting a special act of Congress?" her father said as he slumped in his chair.

"We can pray," Tina said. "It helped me find my sandals."

"You're right, Tina," he said.

The weeks went by, with every Mennonite talking about being sent back to Mexico. There were rumors and gossip, both of which are never good.

It was a Monday afternoon when her father returned home. He was excited. The Friday newspaper had a picture of little girls sitting in class praying. One of them was Tina.

Photos of the blonde-haired, blue-eyed children made it into newspapers across the United States. Suddenly, American citizens were calling and writing letters to the government to let the Mennonites stay.

"I can't believe a photo has changed things," Tina's mother said.

"It has," her father replied. "People can see what's happening here. We don't have our land. The money we paid to one lawyer was wasted, yet we're still in Seminole because God wants us here."

Months later, Tina learned that many caring citizens, along with Texas congressmen and two senators, were all fighting hard to make a pathway for the Mennonites to stay. So it wasn't hard to believe when her father got an important call one evening.

"Yes," he said, his voice shaking. "That's wonderful news. I'll tell my family."

"What is it?" her brother asked.

"President Jimmy Carter just signed a special bill granting more than 500 Mennonites a green card. All these Americans, starting with our Mayor Clark all the way up to the President of the United States of America, have worked faithfully for us so that we can stay in America, even though we are **STRANGERS** in this land."

"What's a green card?" Tina asked.

"It gives someone the right to stay in this country. After five years, you can apply for full citizenship."

"Were our names on that list?" Tina's mother asked.

"They were! Mine, yours, David's, Elizabeth's, Tina's, and Nancy's."

"Yay!" everyone yelled. "We're going to be citizens!"

Sure enough, a week later, their green cards arrived in the mail, one for each Rempel family member. God had answered their prayers.

Chapter Ten

"For our citizenship is in heaven, from which we also eagerly wait for the Savior, the Lord Jesus Christ."
—Philippians 3:20

October 31, 1986

Five years later, Tina had a lot to be thankful for. She had two new brothers, Jacob and Henry. Because they'd been born in the United States, they were automatically citizens.

She also had steady work cleaning houses with her mother.

Tina's father was employed in construction. He made good money and had steady work.

Because of their success, the Rempels had bought a larger, three-bedroom mobile home and added an extra bedroom to it. The family had plenty of room to spread out for their six children and two adults—at least for Mennonites.

"Are you ready?" Tina's mother asked.

"Almost," Tina replied. Tina studied herself in the mirror. She could hardly believe that she was seventeen years old already. Of course, she had outgrown her favorite purple sandals, but she still had them sitting in the closet. Those

purple sandals had traveled a long way with Tina. She could never part with them.

An hour later, the entire family stood in the junior high auditorium. The auditorium bustled with all the Mennonites. A federal judge and other important people sat on the stage, ready for the ceremony to start.

When it came time to say the oath, Tina got to her feet and stood next to her family as they raised their hands to repeat the oath. Next to Tina was her mother and father, her sisters, Elizabeth and Nancy, and her brother, David.

Mayor Bob Clark got to see the fruit of all his hard work in keeping the Mennonites in Seminole.

As the judge spoke, the Rempel family repeated out loud that they promised to support and defend the U.S. Constitution

and the laws of this great country. It took a minute or so until the judge pronounced them U.S. citizens. It was a very happy day.

Back at the mobile home, they had a special supper. After everyone had finished eating, Tina, Elizabeth, and Nancy cleaned up. Once they were done, Tina went outside and found her parents enjoying the sunset.

"Mom and Dad, what are you thinking about?" Tina asked.

Dad turned to Tina. "I just realized that we're no longer strangers in this land. This is our country now."

"That's good, isn't it?" Tina asked.

"Yes," her father replied. "It's just that we have been forced to move from country to country for hundreds of years. I do hope this is our last move."

"We are free here," Tina said. "We can worship freely. We can buy property. We can get educated. This is the best place."

"Yes, it is," her parents said.

"Mom and Dad, thanks for bringing us up out of Mexico. It was hard living there, but you have made our lives better."

"I know that," her mother said. "I just hope you tell your children and grandchildren this story. Make sure they love this country as we do. Raise them to be good citizens not

only of this country but also show them the pathway to our **_HEAVENLY CITIZENSHIP_**."

"Don't worry, Mom and Dad," Tina said. "You can count on me.

They smiled.

The End... of the story, but the beginning of a wonderful life in America!

On November 3, 2019, Tina was invited to come to Plains, Georgia, to meet President Jimmy Carter at his home church.

Tina gave the President and Mrs. Jimmy Carter a copy of her book *SEMINOLE: Some People Never Give Up* as a thank you for signing the law making her and her family citizens of the United States of America.

Tina wasn't wearing her purple sandals. But she couldn't have made it without them. They were the little sandals that could.

Of course, God really did it. He can do anything!

Timeline of John and Tina Siemen's Lives

1941 — Anna Friesen is born on August 2 in Chihuahua, Mexico

1946 — David Rempel is born on May 7 in Chihuahua, Mexico

1965 — David Rempel and Anna Friesen get married on August 15 in Chihuahua, Mexico

1969 — Tina Rempel is born on January 10 in Chihuahua, Mexico

1970 — John Siemens is born on July 26 in Chihuahua, Mexico

1977 — Tina Rempel and her parents move to Seminole, Texas on March 26

1985 — John Siemens and his parents move to Seminole, Texas on March 15

1986 — The Rempel family becomes U.S. citizens on October 31 in Seminole, Texas

1987 — Christina Anne Wiebe is born on May 30 in Andrews, Texas

1988 — John Siemens and Tina Rempel get married on April 17 in Seminole, Texas

1989 — Jonathan Lee Siemens is born on April 13 in Winnipeg, Manitoba, Canada

1989 — Tina Loewen is born on April 13 in Chihuahua, Mexico

1991 — Christopher Lee Siemens is born on August 15 in Andrews, Texas

2006 — John and Jonathan Siemens take their first solo flight on September 5 in Seminole, Texas

2008 — Chris Siemens takes his first solo flight on July 30 in Seminole, Texas

2008 — Jonathan and Tina get married on November 15 in Seminole, Texas

2011 — Bryleigh Kaye Siemens is born October 12 in San Angelo, Texas

2011 — Kira Lynn Siemens is born on October 25 in Seminole, Texas

2012 — Chris and Christy get married on September 1 in Lubbock, Texas

2013 — Kaden Lee Siemens is born on October 16 in Seminole, Texas

2014 — Hudson Lee Siemens is born on April 18 in Lubbock, Texas

2019 — Tina Siemens launches her first book *Seminole: Some People Never Give Up* on September 29 in Seminole, Texas

2022 — Tina Siemens launches her second book *The Little Sandals That Could,* a children's book

Oct. 24, 2021

Met President Jimmy and Rosalynn Carter Nov. 3, 2019

Acted in Book Trailer of Seminole: Some People Never Give Up. Mar. 25, 2019

1st American Doll Oct. 21, 2017

1st day of school Aug. 28, 2017 in Idalou Texas

They shall mount up with wings like eagles Isaiah 40:31

BRYLEIGH KAYE SIEMENS
Born
October 12, 2011

Met President Jimmy and Rosalynn Carter Nov. 3, 2019

Oct. 24, 2021

1st American Doll Oct. 21, 2017

Acted in Book Trailer of Seminole: Some People Never Give Up. Mar. 25, 2019

1st day of school Aug. 21, 2017 in Seminole Texas

They shall mount up with wings like eagles Isaiah 40:31

KIRA LYNN SIEMENS
Born
October 25, 2011

18

36

Oct. 29, 2021

Moved to Siemens' farm July 11, 2020

1st day of school Aug. 15, 2019 in Seminole Texas

1 year of homeschool due to Covid-19 Aug. 17, 2020

Acted in Book Trailer of Seminole: Some People Never Give Up. Mar. 25, 2019

They shall mount up with wings like eagles Isaiah 40:31

KADEN LEE SIEMENS Born October 16, 2013

Moved to Siemens' farm Nov. 14, 2020

Oct. 29, 2021

1 year of homeschool due to Covid-19 Aug. 17, 2020

1st day of school Aug. 15, 2019 in Seminole Texas

18

Acted in Book Trailer of Seminole: Some People Never Give Up. Mar. 25, 2019

They shall mount up with wings like eagles Isaiah 40:31

36

HUDSON LEE SIEMENS
Born
April 18, 2014

World Events

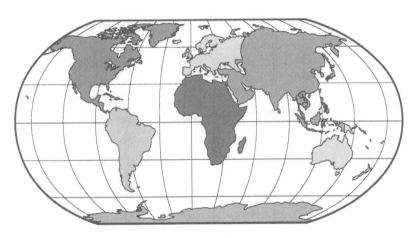

1941 — Japan bombs Pearl Harbor sending the United States into World War II.

1945 — The United States drops two atomic bombs on Japan to end World War II.

1948 — The country of Israel is formally reborn.

1955 — Rosa Parks refuses to give up her seat on a bus and starts begins a civil rights movement.

1959 — Dictator Fidel Castro overthrows the Cuban government and creates a communist one.

1961 — The Berlin Wall is built by the Soviet Union, cutting off West Germany from the rest of the world.

1963 — President John F. Kennedy is assassinated in Dallas, Texas.

1969 — *Apollo XI* lands on the moon, making the United States the first to achieve such a feat.

1974 — President Nixon resigns from the presidency.

1977 — Personal computers burst onto the scene.

1983 — The Internet is born, connecting each person to the world.

1986 — The space shuttle *Challenger* explodes 73 seconds after takeoff.

1989 — The Berlin Wall comes crashing down, reuniting East Germany with West Germany.

1991 — The U.S. goes to war over Kuwait, quickly defeating Iraq.

1993 — The European Union is created, making all of Europe one large economic bloc.

1994 — Jeff Bezos creates Amazon to sell used books.

1995 — Domestic terrorist Timothy McVeigh blows up a federal building in Oklahoma City.

1998 — Google is founded, allowing users to search the world for information.

2001 — Hijackers attack New York City destroying the twin World Trade Center Towers.

2003 — The United States topples Saddam Hussein and his government in Iraq.

2005 — Katrina blows into New Orleans, making it the costliest hurricane in U.S. history.

2007 — The iPhone is invented, allowing users to perform multiple tasks simultaneously.

2009 — Barak Obama becomes the first Black American President.

2016 — Real estate developer and television personality Donald Trump becomes the 45th President.

2019 — China cracks down on Hong Kong, returning the democratic country to authoritarian control.

2020 — The coronavirus pandemic shuts down the world and kills millions.

2021 — The sun continues to come up each morning as U.S. citizens live in a warm freedom and bright prosperity.

Favorite Recipes

Homemade Pizza

Ingredients for Pizza Dough

1	cup of sour milk or cream
1	tablespoon sugar
1	package dry yeast
2	tablespoons butter
2½	cups of flour
1	teaspoon salt
¼	teaspoon baking soda

Instructions:

1. Combine sour milk or cream, sugar, and butter in large sauce pan. Heat to lukewarm. Remove from heat.
2. Add yeast and stir to dissolve.
3. Stir in salt, baking soda, and flour until well blended.
4. Knead dough on floured surface until smooth. Let rest 10 minutes.
5. Pat out and put on desired pizza sauce and toppings. Bake at 400°F for 20 to 30 minutes.
6. Toppings can be any combination, ground beef, salami, pepperoni, and any desired vegetables.
7. One corner can be covered with apple or pear slices sprinkled with sugar and cinnamon as a dessert pizza.

Chocolate Chip Cookies

Ingredients

1	cup shortening
⅔	cup white sugar
⅔	cup brown sugar
2	eggs
1½	cup flour
1	teaspoon salt
1	teaspoon baking soda
1	12 oz package chocolate chips
⅓	cup chopped nuts
1	teaspoon vanilla
2	cups oatmeal

Instructions

1. Cream shortening, then add sugars gradually, add eggs and beat well, add vanilla.
2. Sift flour, salt, and baking soda, and add to creamed mixture.
3. Add nuts, chocolate chips, and oatmeal last.
4. Drop mixture by teaspoonful onto a greased cookie sheet and bake in oven at 350° for 12 minutes.

Kira's favorite

Banana Muffins with Crumb Topping

Ingredients

- 1½ cup all-purpose flour
- 1 teaspoon baking powder
- 1 teaspoon baking soda
- ½ teaspoon salt
- ¾ cup sugar
- 4 large ripe bananas
- 1 large egg slightly beaten
- ⅓ cup of butter melted

Topping

- ⅓ cup packed brown sugar (light or dark)
- 1 tablespoon all-purpose flour
- ½ teaspoon cinnamon
- ¼ cup chopped pecans
- 1 tablespoon cold butter

Muffin Directions
1. In a large bowl, combine the flour, baking soda, baking powder, and salt. Stir with a fork.
2. In a medium-sized bowl, mix the bananas, white sugar, slightly beaten egg, and melted butter together. Pour this mixture into the large bowl with the flour mixture and stir until blended.
3. Fill your paper-lined muffin cups 3/4 full of batter.

Topping Directions
1. In a medium bowl combine the brown sugar, flour, and cinnamon together. Cut the 1 tablespoon of cold butter into the mixture until it's crumbly. Add the chopped pecans and stir.
2. Sprinkle crumb topping on top of muffin batter in pan and bake at 375° for 20 minutes or until toothpick comes out clean. Cool in pan for 10 minutes.

Blender Banana Oatmeal Muffins

Ingredients

2	cups oats—quick-cooking or old fashion
2	large ripe bananas
2	large eggs
1	cup plain nonfat yogurt
3	tablespoons of honey
1½	teaspoons baking powder
½	teaspoon baking soda
½	teaspoon vanilla
½	teaspoon salt
½	cup of either all chocolate chips or dried fruit and nuts mixed

Instructions

1. Preheat oven to 400°F.
2. Lightly grease a 12-cup standard muffin tin or if using liners, lightly grease them as well.
3. Place the ingredients—oats, bananas, eggs, yogurt, honey, baking powder, baking soda, vanilla, and salt—in a blender or food processor fitted with a steel blade.
4. Blend the ingredients once or twice as needed until the batter is smooth and the oats have broken down almost completely—about three minutes.
5. By hand, stir in the nuts, dried fruit, and chocolate chips.
6. Divide the batter among the prepared muffin cups, filling each no more than 3/4 of the way to the top, and sprinkle with additional chocolate chips or nuts if desired.
7. Bake for 15 minutes until the tops of the muffins are set and a toothpick inserted in the center comes out clean.
8. Place the pan on a wire rack and let the muffins cool in the pan for 10 minutes. They will deflate but still taste delicious. Remove from pan and enjoy!

Family Memories

The family at Siemens' farm in Seminole, Texas.

Upper row l to r: Chris, John (Opa), Jonathan;
Lower row l to r: Kira, Christy, Kaden, Tina (Oma), Hudson,
Tina, Bryleigh.

Hudson stirring up dinner

Kaden is pouring a cup of coffee

Bryleigh and Kira makin' cookies.

Hudson, Opa, and Kaden eating the cookies that the girls made

Girls...
and their
dolls...

Kira is sewing her own project.

Bryleigh is getting the details under control.

Hudson is sewing a pillowcase with Oma.

Kaden is sewing a pillowcase with Oma.

Everyone is enjoying a game of Connect Four.

A Mennonite Card Game.
A Vonderful Goot Game!

My Dad's Family Tree

My Mom's Family Tree

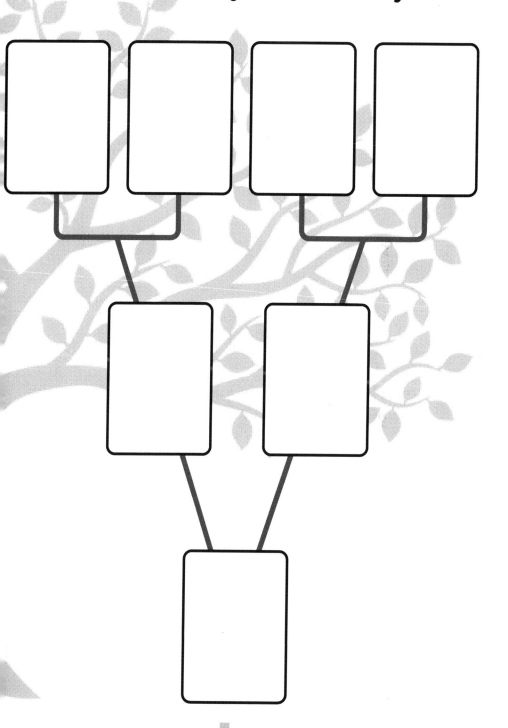

Coloring pages

Enjoy coloring these pages. Adding color to 'The Little Sandals' story will enhance your memories of the adventure Tina had with purple sandals.

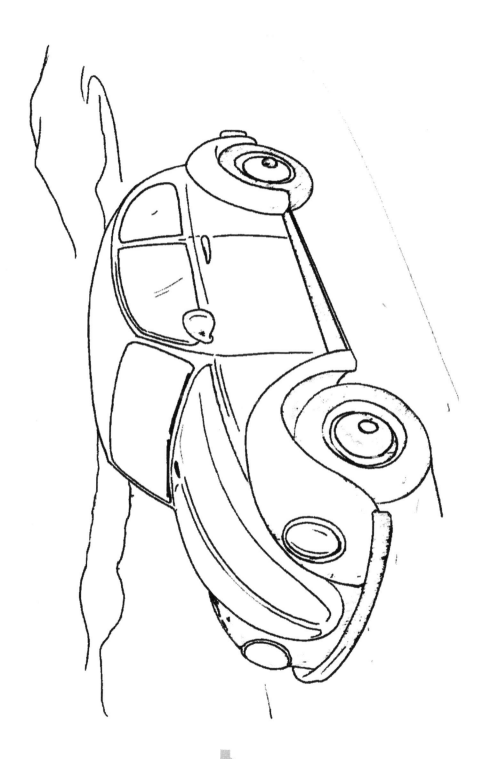

Made in the USA
Middletown, DE
25 October 2022

13415952R00059